My Teen and me.

20 meaningful questions to ease your frustration, build trust, communicate, and connect with your teen.

NANCY BENITEZ

Author Name
Nancy Benitez

Published by Art of Attraction
www.aoa.wtf/myteenandme

[My Teen and me] / [Nancy Benitez] —Ist ed.
ISBN [979-8-2I8-I0553-2]

Ordering Information:
Quantity sales. Special discounts are available on quantity purchases by
corporations, associations, and others. For details, contact us at
www.aoa.wtf/contact

The information presented is the author's opinion and does not constitute
any health or mental health advice. The content of this book is for
informational purposes only and is not intended to diagnose, treat, cure, or
prevent any condition or disease. Please seek advice from your mental
healthcare provider for you or your teen's personal mental health concerns
prior to taking advice from this book.

Dedication

To my mama, who taught me what I needed to know in 16 years, and to my kind, beautiful, and courageous daughter Sadie, who picked up where she left off. I love you with all my heart and soul.

To parents everywhere

"Don't be afraid to make mistakes or to say the wrong thing. You have never parented this teen, at this age, at your age now. So be compassionate, loving, patient, and kind to you both." -Nancy

Introduction

When I turned 16, my brother and I lost our mama to leukemia.

Life after that and into my 20s was chaos. Full of bad decisions, terrible relationships, self-hate, and depression. In order to cope with my mother's death I turned to bulimia, suicidal thoughts, and gangs for comfort. All of this while attempting to raise my 14-year-old brother who became addicted to drugs and toxic friends. He eventually ended up in jail.

My dad was doing his best while grieving my mom, the love of his life. Working nights to care for two teens, he was never around or someone we could turn to for comfort or emotional support.

For an entire year after her death, I vividly remember rummaging through every paper that I could find in our house in hope of finding a letter from her. A love letter where I could read the words "I love you, Nancy. You're going to be okay." A letter that asked the right questions and gave me answers to help me get through the pain and what I should do next! I never found anything. This was one of the hardest times in my life not only because I lost my mom, but because I was left to figure out teen life challenges all on my own.

The reason I'm telling you this story is to let you know that your teen needs you. It doesn't matter if you are blood-related if you're their mother, father, grandparent, caretaker, aunt, uncle, or friend. They need your support and patience to guide them especially when they make mistakes. They need you to ask those loving, difficult, thought-provoking questions that will help them think outside the box and also make sense of things. They want to feel seen, heard, loved, and know that they matter as the capable beings that they are while figuring out what it means to be a good human.

This is your guide to asking your teen those questions that will help build more trust and open up communication so that you don't feel like strangers from different planets.

These are 20 important and meaningful questions that were compiled over the last 32 years by my teen self, my parent self, other teens, parents, coaches, clients, and friends.

I can't promise this guide will solve all of your problems or answer all of your questions. I can say that it's a powerful start to getting to the next level of connection with your teen. I've included some great resources that will offer support and help you make sense of some of the most important subjects in your teen's life today.

You are extraordinary.

I love you and your effort.

I am grateful for you and your courageous heart.

x, Nancy

How to use this book

Asking is easy. Listening without the need to speak, tell, nag, talk down to, or remind is the most difficult part of parenting. Every human on this planet has different realities, priorities, and points of view so remember that there is more than one way of seeing and doing things.

Remember 5 Secrets

Secret #I: Retrain Your Brain
Right now, you get to make a conscious choice to begin retraining your brain by using positive communication with your teen most of the time. When we feel negative emotions, give in to them, and react, we trigger primal genes and see our kids as predators that we need to fight, flee, or hide to feel safe from. Our teens then begin to mirror our behavior and we enter into a battle that no one wins. Begin modeling the behavior you want to see from your teen.

Secret #2: Welcoming Asks
Ask your teen one of the 20 questions or any questions with a positive tone and relaxed, open, and welcoming body language. Be welcoming and confident in your asking and always listen with intent.

Secret #3: Deep Listening
Deep listening means that you are completely present with your child. You're not thinking about dinner, work, or what you have to do tomorrow. It means that after asking a question you try your best to understand them without interrupting or giving advice.

Secret #4: Curiosity
Invite more information from your teen. After asking a question and listening to their answer, you can say "I'm curious, could you tell more about that?" to keep the conversation going. Ask "Is there anything else?" Then feel free to ask if you can share your experience.

Secret #5: Express Gratitude
Always end the conversation with appreciation and gratitude. Thank your child for being open and sharing with you.

Remember, teens, do better when they feel better and so do you!

TABLE OF CONTENTS

1. Do you need me to listen, do you need suggestions or do you need my help?

This question gives you superpowers. Try asking it when your teen comes to you with a problem, an issue, or wants to share something important. Practice asking until it becomes a habit. Honor their request without the need to add your input, and you will begin to experience positive shifts in the conversation and your relationship!

WRITING PROMPT

How would you feel if your partner, teen, or friends asked you this question about an important issue you brought to them?
Write it below, then practice asking it to your teen.

2. I noticed you were upset/
frustrated/angry/sad/mad.

Would you like to talk more about what
happened to upset you? It sounds like it was
really hard for you.

*If they don't want to talk you can say something like "When
you're ready to talk, let me know and I'm happy to listen.
I love you!

Sometimes teens don't want to talk about how they feel because they're trying to figure it out themselves, especially when negative emotions come up. If they don't respond, don't push them. Be present, and loving, and allow them to come to talk to you when ready.

WRITING PROMPT

You know your teen better than anyone! Write a new never tried approach below. Make it an intention to ask it 3 times this week to your teen, your partner, or a friend when you see they're upset.

3. Would you like to share the best or the worst part of your day with me?

I would love to hear all about it when you're ready. If not, that's fine too.

After a few minutes of silence and allowing my daughter to process the events of her day, I ask her this question on our way home. Some days she doesn't want to share and some she asks "Mom, would you like to hear about my day?" She then shares the best, the worst, and everything in between. The key: Be excited to see your kids even if you had a bad day. Try deep listening rather than trying to give advice, nag, or fix. Otherwise, they won't want to share what's important.

WRITING PROMPT

Imagine yourself as a teen. What is one thing you wish your parents would have done or asked you after a long day at school? Write it below and try asking or doing it with your teen.

4. I know homework is hard to do after an entire day at school.

What do you think about setting up a routine to help you?

I am looking at my schedule, and I can be available from _____ to _____, on_____ to help you or sit with you for moral support!

This can be tough for us because we want our teens to excel, so we nag, demand, talk down to, and remind them of their duties. Think for a moment about your current home or work duties. Would you like the added stress of someone constantly nagging, demanding, and talking down to you to do it? No! Our teens don't either and they know that if they don't do it, there will be natural consequences that they'll have to deal with. Allow them to fail, make mistakes, and grow. Adding stress will only cause them to resent you. Teens do better when they feel better. Set aside time to help them and follow through. If they say no, allow them to fail and deal with the consequences.

WRITING PROMPT

Do you have a strategy for getting things done? If so, write down 3 steps and then share them with your teen so they can learn from you. If not, google George T. Doran, founder of SMART goals for free content.

5. I noticed that you are really upset/angry/frustrated/sad/hurt about what happened between your dad/mom and me.

I really care about you and would like to take the time to listen to how you're feeling.

Would you like to talk now or find some time this week?

DIVORCE

Teens can learn that they are completely capable of handling whatever emotions, feelings, and challenges life throws at them with positive guidance, encouragement, expression, and courage. They can see the opportunity to learn and grow from any experience instead of seeing problems as failures.

WRITING PROMPT

Write down 3 strengths that helped you get through a really challenging time in your life. What did you do to overcome it and share it with your teen? Be the hero in your story. If you barely survived through it, look back and ask yourself "What 3 strengths would have helped me in hindsight then share it with your teen.

6. I want you to know that you did nothing wrong to cause the divorce and it's not your fault.
Do you feel that you have to choose between loving and spending time with your mom/dad/parent and me? And why?

DIVORCE

After 18 years in a relationship, I got divorced. One day, in conversation with my daughter, I learned that she felt as though she had to pick between loving my former husband and me. It broke my heart and I told her she didn't have to pick because we both loved her. Allow your teen to like the other parent. Make it okay to like the other parent. And if you don't like them, so what? It's not about you. You liked them at some point. Our kids should be allowed to love both parents equally without having to take sides or feel guilty.

WRITING PROMPT

Think back to when you met your (ex)partner. Below list 3-5 good qualities about them that you can talk about with your teen. Remember "If you can't say something nice, don't say nothin' at all." -" Thumper", Disney's Bambi

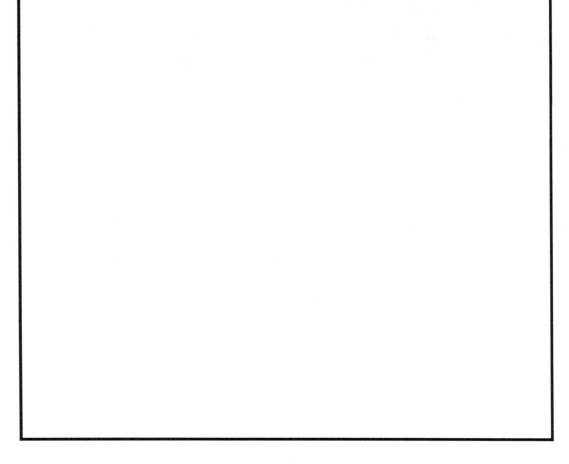

7. What qualities do you look for in a friend and what things are really important for you to have in a friendship?

HEALTHY RELATIONSHIPS

Teens are not born knowing how to have good relationships. They learn it from us and others they observe. This is a great opportunity to understand and LISTEN to what friendship means to your teen from their perspective. This is not the time to tell them what you think, so keep listening and asking if they can tell you more so you know what is going on in their mind.

Once they are done, you can ask if you can share how values like honesty, trust, mutual respect, open communication, consent, and others are important to you in a friendship.

WRITING PROMPT

Below write 5-10 values that are most important for you to have in a friendship then share them with your teen.

8. What things do you look for in a partner/gf/bf/other? Let's make a list of 10 things.

Some great things to include asking your teen are: How do you want them to treat you and talk to you? How would they show you that they loved and cared about you? Are they kind, respectful, and confident, and do they love themselves? What qualities do you look for in a bf/gf/other and what things are really important for you to have in a relationship?

HEALTHY RELATIONSHIPS

This is a huge and sometimes scary topic for us to talk to our kids about. Think about what a good relationship means to you before you ask your teen. As always, remember to ask and listen first. Be silly, and make it fun.

WRITING PROMPT

Below write what values and non-negotiables you want or have with your partner. What are some "red flags" and "hard nos"? How do you feel loved? How do you want a partner to communicate with you? Etc.

9. It's time to talk about family chores and responsibilities. Who would like the opportunity to write this week's list and who would like to commit to doing what?

RESPONSIBILITIES

Teens need boundaries, agreements, and guidelines when it comes to chores, responsibilities, and even homework. Creating an agreement is simple. Here are 5 steps to guide you.

I. Create a list: Your family needs to get clear on what needs to be done for the week through a kind, firm, and loving conversation. Brainstorm together a list of all the chores that need to be done in a weekly family meeting.

2. Schedule time blocks: Come up with realistic days and times with your teen to do chores, homework, etc. Inform them of the weekly activities you have going on and then allow them to set their own times for their responsibilities down to the minutes. You each have different priorities.

3. Keep it in plain sight: Have your teen put their list somewhere visible in their space or on a calendar. If it's out of sight, it's out of mind.

4. Consequences: Agree on what will happen if they don't follow through on what they committed to. Come up with ideas you both agree on.

5. Follow through: Follow through but don't nag, demand, yell, or engage in a power struggle. Instead, when you notice they didn't follow through on the agreed time, stop them from what they are doing to get their attention, and say in a calm and kind voice "Do you remember our agreement?" If they don't remember, ask them to look at their calendar. If they still don't do what they said, follow through on #4! Be strong, and stay committed, they will eventually get it after a few times of you following through.

WRITING PROMPT

Write down a time that works for you and your family to go over chores for the next 4 weeks, then use steps I-5.

10. You made a mistake/accident/
unfortunate decision. We all do.

Would you like my help in coming up with 3
solutions to correct this mistake/
accident?

RESPONSIBILITIES

Mistakes are opportunities to learn, grow and expand our consciousness. After the incident occurs, as an adult calm your mind first, and ask yourself "Am I reacting from a place of fear, anxiety, or anger or from love and encouragement?" Teens deserve to be treated with compassion and respect. Remember, they are doing their best with the limited years of experience they have. When you are calm, share what's important to you and why, and have your teen do the same. See them as powerful beings capable of learning from their mistakes.

WRITING PROMPT

Ask yourself, how do I like to be treated when I make a mistake? Then below, list 3 mistakes, you have made as a parent, what you learned, and the solutions that helped you get through them. Share with your teen to create an open and loving connection.

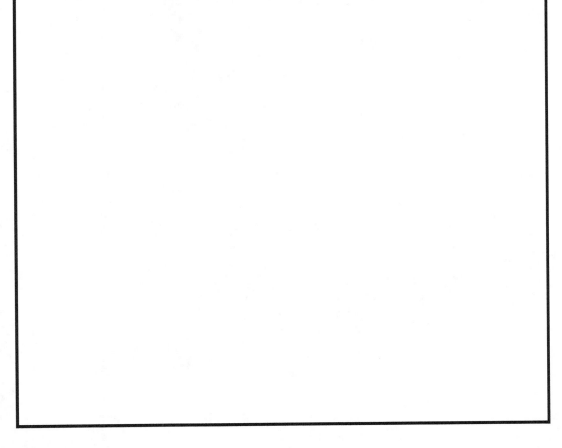

11. What is something you would like others to appreciate or notice about you?

GRATITUDE AND APPRECIATION

Do you like to feel appreciated? So do our teens. They enjoy feeling accomplished and being complimented even though they act like they don't care. When you notice something kind your teen did, said, or worked really hard on, ask if you can share what you noticed. Give them a compliment and be specific about what you noticed instead of saying the token "Good job!"

WRITING PROMPT

Below, write 3 things your teen did this past week where you thought "Wow that was really cool, I'm so proud of them." Then ask if you can share it with them.

12. What are 3 things that you are grateful for today?

GRATITUDE AND APPRECIATION

Our teens are running on high emotions due to so much pressure and change in their brain and their body. Taking time to connect in the morning for a couple of minutes in verbalizing the good things in your life together will help create a connection. If your teen is grouchy and can't seem to be grateful, that's okay. I encourage you as a parent to keep it going every day and share it with them. They will come around.

WRITING PROMPT

What are 3 things that you are grateful for today and why? Write them below and share them with your teen:

13. When you're ready, would you like to talk about how you're feeling? I can answer your questions the best that I can to help you through grieving.

No matter how it happens, death is truly painful this also applies to our pets. It's especially hard for teens who don't have all the skills to process it yet. They may have a lot of unanswered questions and feelings that they're dealing with. They need someone close to them to affirm and let them know that it's okay to grieve and feel sadness, anger, anxiety, guilt, or despair and at other times feel happy, joyful, and good too. Sometimes they may not know how they are feeling and it can be confusing.

Some ways you can help your teen if they are not willing to talk to you are to find other teen groups who have had similar experiences. Find a grief counselor, or have them talk to another close friend who is a parent.

WRITING PROMPT

Below, write 3 ways you managed your own grief in the past that you found helpful in moving forward, then share it with your teen if they are open to it.

14. This is a really hard time in your life and you're probably wondering how you're going to get through it when you're going to feel better, or what's next. When you want to talk, would you like to come up with some ideas of things to do each day that will help you begin feeling a little bit better each day?

DEATH OF A LOVED ONE

I explained in the introduction that I lost my mom to cancer at the age of 16, so this topic is close to my heart. These two questions will help your teen know it's okay to feel what they are feeling and talk about it. You are also giving them tools to move forward through one of the toughest times in their lives and empowering them to know that they will get through this one day at a time.

WRITING PROMPT

If, as a parent, you are also grieving the loss of a loved one, allow yourself the time to write below how you are feeling right now and some ways you can feel comforted with this loss.

15. I know there may be talk at school or among your friends about self-harm, cutting, and eating disorders. Do you know what these are, what they mean, and how they affect your physical and mental health?

SELF HARM, CUTTING, EATING DISORDERS

When I was a teen, I overheard girls in the bathroom talking about bulimia, so I decided to try it and it lasted 20 years because eating made me happy and I didn't want to be fat. Sadly, my parents didn't know to educate me on the consequences of self harm.

These may be uncomfortable topics to bring up with your teen but I can guarantee that if you educate them and yourself, you will both feel confident and empowered to make better decisions.

WRITING PROMPT

Go online and google "How can self-harm affect a growing teen's body, brain, and mental health." Write 3 key things below that resonated with you and discuss them with your teen.

16. Are you okay? Would you like to talk to me or someone you trust about how you are feeling about yourself and your body?

SELF HARM, CUTTING, EATING DISORDERS

When I was a teen, I overheard girls in the bathroom talking about bulimia, so I decided to try it and it lasted 20 years because eating made me happy and I didn't want to be fat. Sadly, my parents didn't know to educate me on the consequences of self harm.

These may be uncomfortable topics to bring up with your teen but I can guarantee that if you educate them and yourself, you will both feel confident and empowered to make better decisions.

WRITING PROMPT

Go online and google "How can self-harm affect a growing teen's body, brain, and mental health." Write 3 key things below that resonated with you and discuss them with your teen.

17. Do you feel safe at school and have you heard what being a victim of prejudice, violence, sexting, or cyberbullying means?

(If you do, I would like to listen to learn more about what you know and if you have any questions.)

BULLYING: PREJUDICE, VIOLENCE, SEXTING, CYBERBULLYING, OR OTHER SAFETY ISSUES

Take the time to talk to your teen about bullying and their concerns if you haven't already. Brainstorm solutions with your teen and your entire family about possible solutions if they are experiencing some form of bullying. By doing something with their problem, your teen will experience a feeling of control and empowerment. This encourages personal responsibility and builds life skills. Rather than protecting or rescuing your teen from difficult situations, assist them in planning a strategy that will help them overcome their challenge. If your teen doesn't ask for help, it is up to you to be aware and intervene in the problem. You as a parent know when something is wrong with your teen. Remind them that you are on their side and willing to help them with any problem they may face.

WRITING PROMPT

Below, brainstorm solutions with your teen about what they can do or will do if they encounter bullying, and invite the whole family to come up with solutions to create a deeper connection. If you, as a parent, are unsure of what to do, remember you are not alone. Please get help from your school, community, or a restorative justice program.

18. Did you know that you have choices and unlimited power over your words and your actions?

BULLYING: PREJUDICE, VIOLENCE, SEXTING, CYBERBULLYING, OR OTHER SAFETY ISSUES

Explain to your teen that when someone treats them in a mean or hurtful way, it's their job to either state their needs clearly or to leave the situation with dignity.
Invite them to role-play situations with you.

WRITING PROMPT

Below, write 3 scenarios where you, your family, and your teen can role-play difficult situations. This will help them feel empowered to stand up and use their voice when/if it happens. If your teen is shy, role play with someone else who is willing and explain to your teen that this will prepare them for a real-life situation.

19. Do you feel safe with your friends and on social media and do you know what sexting, porn, grooming, pedophilia, and a digital footprint, are and what the law & criminal consequences are when it comes to sex and sexting are?

SEX AND CONSENT

Teens today have more access to information and have a general idea of what sex is through social media. If your teen does not, please educate them and ask them confidently if they know what sex is. If you don't, someone else at school or online will. This is a tough subject for us parents to talk to our teens about and when we educate our children and give them the tools they need, it empowers them and gives them the confidence to overcome tough challenges.

WRITING PROMPT

Go back in time and think about the conversations, if any, you had with your parents as a teen about sex and any of these topics. What do you wish you had known or they had shared with you? How would you have changed their approach in talking to you about it? Write your experience below, then share it with your teen to create a connection.

20. Do you know what sexual consent is and how drugs and alcohol affect it?

SEX AND CONSENT

When was the last time you asked your teen this question? Again, a
tough one. But necessary. Regardless of beliefs or religion, it's
important to talk to our kids about sex, sexual consent, pleasure,
orgasms, masturbation, their bodies, intimacy, and the joy and
responsibilities of having sex. It is also key that you educate them
about the effects drugs and alcohol have on their common sense and
decision-making skills even if you don't think they will ever drink
or use drugs. Knowledge is power.

WRITING PROMPT

Write down I-2 life experiences you either had or heard about from a
close relative that changed your perspective on sexual consent,
drugs, and alcohol. If you're comfortable share it with your teen.

RESOURCE BOOK LIST

Positive Discipline for Teenagers

Positive Discipline for teenagers by Jane Nelsen and Lynn Lott teaches important social and life skills in a manner that is deeply respectful and encouraging for both children and adults.

positivediscipline.com

Brainstorm: The Power and Purpose of the Teenage Brain

In this New York Times-bestselling book, Dr. Daniel Siegel shows parents how to turn one of the most challenging developmental periods in their children's lives into one of the most rewarding.

drdansiegel.com

Learning How to Learn: For Kids and Teens

How to Succeed in School Without Spending All Your Time Studying. The bestseller A for kids and teens to teach them simple tricks to learn difficult subjects—whether they feel like good students or not.

barbaraoakley.com/books/learning-how-to-learn/

Perfect Health for Kids Book

Little-known secrets every parent should know by Dr. John Douillard using time-tested and scientifically-proven Ayurvedic principles, parents can do more than just treat symptoms; they can get to the root cause of childhood and teen weight gain, ADD, asthma, allergies, hormones, stomach aches and more.
https://store.lifespa.com/

RESOURCE COACH LIST

Sheri Gazitt, M.A. | Girl Drama Parent Teen Coach

Sheri is passionate about empowering parents and teens through their adolescent years. She advocates for teen mental wellness and provides private coaching for teens who need help reclaiming their confidence, learning new relationship skills, and navigating friendships. Her superpower is empowering girls going through friendship shifts or girl drama.

Go to: TeenWiseSeattle.com and FB:facebook.com/groups/theparentinglab

Amy Lang | Sex Educator | Workshops | Consults

Through her company Bird & Bees & Kids, Amy Lang, MA helps parents become their kid's go-to birds and bees expert. Through her podcast, Just Say This, and book Sex Talks With Tweens: What to Say & How to Say It, she has helped thousands of parents and caregivers around the world rock the sex talks.

Go to: birdsandbeesandkids.com and FB:facebook.com/birdsbeeskids

Philip Turner | Divorce Coach

Philip is a divorce coach who specializes in helping men and women release themselves from past conditioning so they can quickly adjust to their new lives as individuals or single parents. His approach accelerates the healing process and helps parents show up in a powerful way for their teens.

To schedule a time to talk with him I-I, go to www.philipturner.youcanbook.me

Casey O'Roarty | Parent Coach

You are not living in your own private freak show. This is a collective experience. It's okay to reach out for help. In fact, it's pretty admirable and a great model for your children.

Go to: https://www.besproutable.com/teens/ and FB: www.facebook.com/joyfulcourage

RESOURCE PODCAST LIST

JOYFUL COURAGE PODCAST: PARENTING JOURNEY

A conscious parenting podcast. This is a weekly show that is designed to entertain and inform as I tease apart all there is to learn on the parenting journey. Interviews are packed full of useful nuggets for parents to take away and integrate into their own experiences.

www.besproutable.com/podcasts

JUST SAY THIS PODCAST: SEXUALITY

I'm on a mission to help every kid grow up to be a whole healthy adult! I do this by helping parents just like you learn how to have open and effective talks about sexuality!

birdsandbeesandkids.com/category/podcast/

THE ULTIMATE HEALTH PODCAST: HEALTH

This podcast focuses on the development of mindsight and teaches insight, empathy, and integration in individuals, families and communities. Author of Brainstorm: The Power and Purpose of the Teenage Brain and No Drama discipline.

ultimatehealthpodcast.com/dr-dan-siegel/

WELLNESS MAMA PODCAST: NATURAL LIVING

A weekly podcast series covering the health topics of real food, stress, sleep, fitness, toxins, natural living, and much more to give you actionable steps to improve your family's health.

https://wellnessmama.com/podcast/

RESOURCE WEBSITE LIST

SUPER HEALTHY KIDS: HEALTHY LIVING

Sharing home-cooked meals create happy memories and healthy habits for life. Full of thoughtfully created routines surrounding food, sleep, and exercise that help kids thrive. Parents can make a big impact on their kids' future well-being by making small positive changes today.

www.superhealthykids.com/

SOUND DISCIPLINE WORKSHOPS: TRAUMA & SUPPORT

Parenting courses that teach skills that will help parents build positive relationships with children who have experienced trauma and focus on strategies that encourage accountability while maintaining connection and more.

www.sounddiscipline.org/workshops/

THE 5 LOVE lANGUAGES FOR TEENS

Socially, mentally, and spiritually, teenagers face pressures and stresses each day. Despite these pressures, it is still parents who can influence teens the most. This book by Gary Chapman shows parents to make the most of the opportunity.

5lovelanguages.com

WELLNESS MAMA

Simple Answers for Healthier Families. We believe that moms are the most powerful force on the planet and we're unwavering in supporting, uplifting, and encouraging each other.

https://wellnessmama.com/

MY PARENTING WINS!

I WILL MIRROR WHAT I DESIRE

MY PARENTING CHALLENGES?

PARENTING IS EXPANDING MY HEART AND SOUL

NEW PARENTING IDEAS.

WHEN I DO GOOD I FEEL GOOD

QUESTIONS I WANT TO ASK MY TEEN?

I WILL REFLECT WHAT I DESIRE

MISTAKES I SAW AS OPPORTUNITIES.

I AM COURAGEOUS AND CAPABLE

THOUGHTS & FEELS

I AM PURE LOVE

THANK YOU FROM MY ♥ TO YOURS

A FREE GIFT FOR YOU!

GO TO WWW.AOA.WTF/MYTEENANDME

I AM ENOUGH

CPSIA information can be obtained
at www.ICGtesting.com
Printed in the USA
BVHW021027010223
657603BV00013B/54